15/-
75 n.p.

Alasdair Ramsay

DAVID COLEMAN'S
WORLD
OF
FOOTBALL

DAVID COLEMAN'S WORLD OF FOOTBALL

REPORTER   NORMAN HARRIS

PURNELL
London W.1

CONTENTS

THE FATAL FASCINATION....

On the athletic track, Lillian Board closes with Collette Besson.

Lillian Board was running for Britain in the 4×400-metre relay at the 1969 European Games in Athens. In a sensational final-leg confrontation with the Olympic champion from France, Collette Besson, she saw the French girl race away and set up a lead of 20 yards. As they turned into the home straight all of that distance remained between them; Miss Besson's gamble was about to be crowned with success. Lillian Board began to close the gap, but the chase seemed futile. At the end she was coming very, very fast —but the French girl, though slowing badly, was on the very brink of the tape. In those last five yards Lillian Board got there—and it was only *then* that it seemed believable . . . And perhaps even then, not all that believable. Says Lillian Board: "I've seen the film of that race a dozen times, and each time I see it I can't believe that I'm going to win. I'm sure that one day when I watch that film I *won't* win!"

THAT THESE SCENES SHARE

At Wembley, an Everton fan evades a police tackle.

The Everton fan—a famous figure— is celebrating Trebilcock's equalising goal in the 1966 Cup Final against Sheffield Wednesday. His joy was understandable, since only six minutes previously Everton were 0 – 2 down and the game was two-thirds over. Low-rated Sheffield Wednesday were exerting calm and authoritative control over the favourites. Springett, further-more, was in impeccable form in the Wednesday goal . . . Then, suddenly, Trebilcock hit home. Five minutes later he did it again. In another ten minutes, Everton's winning third was in the net: three goals in 16 minutes. A final, so said the F.A.'s own report, to rank with the 'Matthews' final of 1953, for the "dramatic recovery of an ap-parently beaten team." There's a film of that, too, and every time they show it at Everton more and more people pack in to watch it. Some of them keep coming back to see it, so a story goes, because they're really waiting for the day when Everton lose that match.

ARE YOU LISTENING STRETFORD END?

They say that Manchester United is a unique team, and that what makes it unique is something indefinable, some sort of magic that has to do with tradition and individual character. At least, that's what Geoffrey Godbert says. He's a 32-year-old public relations man in London, but he's also a United fan who sees every match that United plays— as he has done, year in and year out, since he was eight. He says that the Stretford Enders *of today have it all wrong. United's 'unbeatable ability to entertain' is in fact the character and the tradition of Yesterday.*

It's fairly easy for most club supporters to remember their team's best performances. Or name their best players since the war. Because it doesn't take a long time to skim the cream of success off the milk of mediocrity. And that's the case with nearly all British teams. Including Leeds.

But it's less easy with Manchester United. My team. When the Stretford End recently chose a lad from their ranks to rush onto the Old Trafford pitch and put a paper crown on the head of Brian Kidd, another United 'King' was born. The deposed head was Denis Law, at the same time sadly nursing an old injury. Not that United's general supporters had forgotten Denis. Who could? But the Stretford End lives only for today, and today's successes. *Stretford Enders* are too young to have much room for memories.

They don't realise what they're missing. The current United team doesn't enjoy the highest match attendances in Britain for nothing. The Stretford End, in explanation, would undoubtedly point the finger at the world reputations of George Best, Bobby Charlton, Denis Law and Nobby Stiles, and the fast-rising stars of players like Brian Kidd. To an obvious degree all that is true. But it should be equally true, for example, of the current Leeds team. Yet, no matter what the reputations of Bremner, Hunter, Jackie Charlton and Clarke, it's a fact that Elland Road is hardly ever filled to capacity.

So, it's clear that to fill a football ground week after week, month after month, year after year, requires a long history of successful results and successful players. That's where Man-

Byrne of the Babes: "skill and ice-cold temperament."

chester United score over all competition. Fans who have known the club since the end of the war, know better than any member of the Stretford End why they support this great team.

For a start there's always been something magical and romantic about them. In 1946 United were a team without a ground. Old Trafford was a war victim. Fans followed them to Huddersfield's ground and Goodison Park to see them play "at home" in the F.A. Cup. And their performances matched up to the expectations of the pilgrims. Anyone at Villa Park for the 3rd Round tie in the 47/48 season, not only saw United win a marvellous ten-goal epic of a game; but were present at the dawn of United's unbeatable ability to entertain the crowd.

This special breed of United "personality" was carried on into the 50s by the Babes. For the first time for a long time, people actually fell in love with a football team. Tommy Taylor's lethal elegance; Duncan Edwards' thrilling power; the uncanny intricacy of Eddie Colman; and the ice-cold temperament and skill of Roger Byrne. These and the rest of the young side were all alike anxiously watched-over,

The Babes, 1958. Back row (left to right) Tom Curry (Trainer), Duncan Edwards, Mark Jones, Ray Wood, Bobby Charlton, Bill Foulkes, Matt Busby. Front row (left to right) Johnny Berry, Billy Whelan, Roger Byrne, David Pegg, E. Coleman.

14

favourite sons and brothers to their fans. They fought their way into Europe. And would have swept through victorious but for Munich. This was the time when United's name took its place on the international reputation lists — the first post-war British club to really make it — alongside Real Madrid and Benfica. And it was a bunch of kids who brought it off. No wonder a city wept when they died.

And to go alongside this background of skill and endeavour, the most important of all United's traditions grew stronger. The fact that the teams of the 40s and 50s won or nearly won everything worth winning in football is only half the story. Only the final outcome of the way the players actually got on with the game. When United beat Blackpool in the 1948 Final, it was a triumph for un-adulterated ability. When United won their first league championship in 1952, no one who saw them during that season will ever forget their play. And the same was true of their entry into Europe. Brilliant player after brilliant player earned United a reputation for making never-to-be-forgotten games. Win, lose or draw. It's the same magic that marks today's team.

Which leads, as always, to the players themselves. Comparisons are always so unfair. But if Bobby Charlton has a hard shot, then Jack Rowley, United's centre-forward of 20 years ago, literally let cannonballs fly. If Crerand is cultivated, then Rowley's captain, Johnny Carey, was his

15

professor — in any position. Alex Step-ney has stopped a few penalty kicks, but Jack Crompton made an even greater habit of it in the early post-war days. And so with the Babes, Blanch-flower, Whelan, Pegg and Co. would have made members of United's cur-rent team breathe a sigh of relief every time they managed to get a first team place.

Yet, it is the United of the 60s which won the ultimate accolade of success; something no other United team could bring home. Europe. And nearly the world. That magnificent May evening at Wembley meant a lot more than a 4—1 victory in the Euro-pean Cup Final. It was bigger than any of the players who actually won the game. It was a triumph for every-thing United have stood for since the war. For the guts of Jimmy Delaney as well as the multi-million pound style of George Best; for the grace of Charlie

Flashback to '57: Tommy
Taylor beats Tottenham's
Marchi and Baker.

Mitten, as well as John Aston's speed; for Henry Cockburn, Johnny Morris and Stan Pearson, as well as the 50s. And for the same unbreakable United that survived Munich.

If that's hard to believe, look in any United programme. The bare facts are there on record. Five post-war league championships; runners-up seven times; twice winners of the F.A. Cup in the same period; twice runners-up; ten times F.A. Cup semi-finalists; four

times European Cup semi-finalists.

But there's much, much more besides. More than a single player's skill. More than one United team's performance. More than their greatest victory. More than their biggest crowd. Or their biggest buy. Or their best find.

It starts in 1945 when Matt Busy left the forces. And carries on, beyond even his knighthood. Right into the future.

Are you listening, Stretford End?

17

PROMISES, PROMISES

Terry Squires is a man with problems. He is 36 years old, an advertising executive, he lives in Chelmsford with his wife and two children, he has a government to support, and West Ham. *As far as West Ham is concerned, there is no turning back now. Having supported them since the age of 12, he is now, as he says, committed to loving and hating them "till death do us part." He has come to terms with his life.* This is his personal testament . . .

When I die, and my whole life flashes before my eyes, I shall remember the 1960's in particular. A large part of that period will be coloured by claret-and-blue flashes intermingled with a mixture of sheer football genius and deep gloom. Second Division Champions and promotion . . . defeat in the Cup by Swindon Town . . . F.A. Cup winners . . . defeat in the Cup by Mansfield Town . . . winners in Europe . . . and defeat in the Cup this season by yet another 2nd Division side, Middlesborough—the final twist of the knife when your father-in-law is a Boro' man and an Arsenal supporter to boot . . . a jumbled mass of memories that will further rub salt into the wounds inflicted by the vagaries of Greenwood's Gremlins.

The last decade in the life and times of this fervent Hammers supporter has been one long series of ups and downs. Next to Michael Parkinson of the *Sunday Times* and his beloved Barnsley, I must be the most frustrated football fanatic in the country. Unlike the present Barnsley side, West Ham undoubtedly have talent. But where the hell does it go most Saturday afternoons? To paraphrase Rex Harrison in *'My Fair Lady'*—"Why can't West Ham be more like Leeds . . . or Everton . . . or Liverpool . . . or . . ." But what's the use? They're not! They're a mixture of sheer genius and comic opera and, it seems, a masochistic desire for self-destruction.

Looking back to the late forties and the early fifties, and my first breathless boyhood days watching the 'Irons' . . . Archie McAuly . . . Ernie Gregory . . . Dick Walker . . . 'Rabbit' Parsons . . . John Dick, and so on . . . I suppose

18

I deserve to suffer. You see, I am a North Londoner and gave my soul to West Ham United to avoid the interminable arguments that went on among my friends about the respective merits of Spurs and Arsenal. I was on safe ground—or so I thought. The Hammers were a middle-of-the-table 2nd Division side, bothering nobody and therefore accepted as such. It didn't seem to matter that they rarely progressed beyond the 4th round of the Cup. And I swear they booked their middle-of-the-league position *before* the season started.

Then a miracle happened, and fortune smiled at last. 1957-58 season saw a quick nip up the league table, and bingo—promotion! A couple of seasons passed placidly enough and then this fellow Ron Greenwood came along (from Arsenal of all places) and taught them a little football . . . and that's when the trouble started. Before I knew where I was the lads had won the F.A. Cup and the European Cup Winners' Cup. The press were talking about my beloved team as trendsetters . . . innovators . . . players of sophistication and intelligence . . . a breath of fresh air . . . playing attractive, attacking football when penalty areas were becoming more crowded than Oxford Circus in the rush hour. It was all too much—not only for the supporters, but also for the team, so it seems.

And since those halcyon days of the mid-sixties, very little has happened to warm the cockles of the heart. True, *we* won the World Cup for England (with a little help from Sir Alf and one or two other players). True, we gave the world three of the greatest players of the decade . . . Bobby Moore—"the OBE", as he is known to the aristocracy of the Chicken Run, Captain of Club and Country, master tactician and one of the world's greatest readers of the game; Geoff Hurst—striker par excellence, exponent of the near post centre (a West Ham innovation now gratefully imitated by the rest of the football world), a player completely unselfish and brilliant in his creation of chances for others from wing positions; Martin Peters, no longer with us I know, but a player rated as one of the best in the world, devastating when coming from behind, master of the quick, incisive wall pass in a crowded penalty area. These are a joy to watch. And true, West Ham have given much to football in terms of managers and coaches . . . Malcolm Allison, Dave Sexton, Frank O'Farrell, Jimmy Bloomfield to name a few . . . all highly talented and highly respected in the game.

But what about today's team? The team that Alf Garnett and I will love, hate, curse and cheer until death do us part. Will they ever change? Will they ever lose their frustrating habit of seeming nonchalance under pressure; of making those awful, silly, defensive errors that are punished so ruthlessly by the opposition? Will they ever punish the opposition's mistakes with the same ruthlessness?

The funny thing is, it doesn't really matter. Like most people who are football daft, I shall go on supporting them with the same mixture of love and hate, joy and tears, until I finally

Which way West Ham? Haphazard or incisive, dominant or disappointing, one fan at least will go on supporting them.

go to that big football stand up in the sky. But I would like them to win *something* occasionally. Then my family, friends and colleagues will have an easier time after the results come in on Saturday evenings. And my three year old son—who has already been brainwashed into believing that Hammers are the greatest, and that he, Bobby Moore, and his Old Man,

are the three best players in the world—will not grow up thinking his father must be out of his tiny mind to follow that bunch of stiffs from Upton Park.

I only hope that the Hammers never sink to the level of Barnsley. I don't think I could show the same fortitude in adversity as Michael Parkinson. (Where the hell is Barnsley, anyway?)

THE BEST GAME OF THE SEASON

Twenty men give twenty different opinions—not a surprising variance, since each of these First Division managers looked back at the season from their own point of view. The question to which they directed their minds was: What was the most satisfying match of the season? Their answers show quite clearly that what they seek is certainly not '2 points at all costs' . . .

EVERTON (Harry Catterick): I think probably the match against West Bromwich Albion was the one, where we clinched the championship. This was the vital one. We weren't to know that we would end up nine points or so clear. We knew it was a vital match and we put a lot of work into preparing for it. There was a lot of interest, a capacity crowd, a lot of tension. And the lads played particularly well and really worked for it and won themselves the two points they got.

*   *   *

LEEDS (Don Revie): I think the one when we beat Everton here, 2−1. Because we'd been to Newcastle the day before and lost 2−1—we'd played fairly well, but lost it. It was Christmas time and we had to pick ourselves off the floor after being beat at Newcastle, to meet Everton, who were our challenge the next day. And in 24 hours the boys picked themselves off the floor and played a really tremendous game. It

was a hard match, right from the off; actually, if we'd got the points at Newcastle we possibly wouldn't have played so well. It was the most satisfying thing that I've ever seen so far.

*   *   *

CHELSEA (Dave Sexton): We'd lost the first two games of the season, away to Liverpool and West Ham, we hadn't got a point, and then we played West Ham again at home here in mid-week. Bobby Tambling did his cartilage in the first 10 minutes and he had to go off, Alan Birchenall came on as substitute, then Ian Hutchinson got concussion about 10 minutes after that and had to go off, so we were down to 10 men, and Marvin Hinton was injured, so that was nine and a half. But we got our first point, we drew 0−0. The boys pulled everything out, it really was a tremendous performance, especially against West Ham who move the ball around so well that if you're short they can expose you. I thought that was the most remarkable performance of the year, really; you remember when you were most vulnerable, and how you overcame it at that time. Maybe the Cup Final performance owed something to that, hauling ourselves up.

*   *   *

DERBY (Brian Clough): We had two or three almost perfect matches this year — we beat Tottenham 5—0, we beat Liverpool 4—0, and then 2—0 at their place — they're not bad starters. These were all very satisfying, but I think, looking back on the season, the most satisfying result would have to be when we beat the side who went on to become League champions. Everton were undefeated in the League, and so were we, after seven games — and we beat them 2—1 at Derby. We played some of our purest football in that match — if that's not too naive a thing to talk about — pure football. I'm sure it's not, if it's associated with Derby.

*   *   *

LIVERPOOL (Bill Shankly): Beating Everton — aye — 3—0 away at Goodison Park. No doubt about it. We played well and we got the result as well. We planned a lot and our plans were borne out. We dominated the match.

SOUTHAMPTON (Ted Bates): We beat Manchester United away 4—1 early in the season. That was probably the best result — our best performance as far as playing is concerned. But when we beat Everton 2—1 at home it was at a vital stage of the season for us. We'd just been knocked out of the Fairs Cup and we needed that result to get our League position on a healthier footing. That was the most satisfying result for us.

*   *   *

IPSWICH TOWN (Bobby Robson): The most satisfying match from our point of view this season was when we beat Arsenal 2—1 here, towards the end of the season in a very fine match — an evening match — when we needed the points to keep us in the First Division. We were one down at half-time, had a couple of injuries as well, and we pulled the game out of the fire in the second half with two marvellously taken personal goals. One of them was by Billy Baxter — captain of the club, it's his testimonial year, and this was his first goal of the season, so it couldn't have happened at a nicer time for him and the club. That made it one-each, and Frank Clarke, the boy we bought from Queen's Park Rangers, scored his first goal for the club—a very fine goal—and that gave us a 2—1 lead, and we finished the match playing ever so well, very competently, very determinedly, and with two points which were invaluable. The crowd got behind us on that day, and the lads responded to it, complemented each other, and in the end we were having a marvellous time.

*   *   *

BURNLEY (Jimmy Adamson): I can't say there was any particular game I was especially satisfied with. One of our outstanding games, though, was against Nottingham when we drew 1—1 there. We also beat them 5—0 at home. But the 1—1 draw was possibly our best performance this season—one of those games where the score-line didn't justify the actual play. We could have won 4-nothing. But they equalised with the last kick of the match. Our performance in that game, overall, was one of the outstanding ones of the year.

*   *   *

NOTTINGHAM FOREST (Matt Gillies): A 1—1 draw at Liverpool was the most satisfying match for me, I think. We played particularly well, exceptionally well, we played some really attacking football in that match, and it wasn't until late in the second half that Liverpool equalised. And a couple of players came back to form— form I hadn't seen them in for the month or so before, and that pleased me as well.

WEST BROMWICH ALBION (Alan Ashman): At the start of the season we'd gone six home matches without winning one of them, then in consecutive home matches we beat Manchester United 2—1 and Everton 2—0. In the previous two home matches we'd struggled to get this win—we drew with Liverpool 2—2, and they scored the equaliser deep into injury time, and that was a disappointment, because we'd played well and should have won the match. Then we drew 1—1 against Leeds at home and played well in that match too. They were punishing matches, several of them at that time. We had to wait until Manchester United, on October 25th, and we played well, and it was a very welcome two points for us. That's the one that sticks in the mind. The worst part of the game is losing at home, and when you don't win at home for several matches it's very, very hard work.

*   *   *

WEST HAM (Ron Greenwood): I think I can say that, basically, I can get satisfaction from every match—the self-satisfaction of playing football, and that's what we're involved in. We had some very frustrating matches, as far as results are concerned; we played very well, really, against Manchester City here and got beat 4—0, and we played well against Everton and got beat 1—0. I suppose the most satisfying one was when we went to Manchester City after we'd just signed Greaves and his first appearance gave the whole side a lift, and we scored five goals. If one's talking about satisfaction that

Greaves joins West Ham and lifts them to 5 goals against Manchester City. For manager Ron Greenwood this was the game of the season.

would be the one. We didn't necessarily play perfect football, but what happened was very pleasing.

* * *

COVENTRY CITY (Noel Cantwell): Most of the games I was satisfied with were away games, because we got as many points away from home as we did at home. We didn't do very well at home really. So the best home wins seem to stand out a bit. A 4—1 win against Southampton was very satisfying. They weren't a difficult side, perhaps, but we played well as a team, we scored four goals and we hadn't scored four at home all season, so this was very gratifying. That was the game we played best in at home, I think. . . . Possibly the game I was most satisfied with was against Arsenal at home. We beat Arsenal 2—0 and it was a tight game, but a battle, and our fellows won it. And we played well. So that would probably be the hardest game and the one that gave me most satisfaction.

* * *

NEWCASTLE UNITED (Joe Harvey): Against Arsenal here, we beat them 3—1. It was Match of the Day as well. Arsenal were doing very well at the time. It was a great game—they contributed as well as us. It was one of those days when everything goes well; the crowd had good entertainment, which you're after, and all the goals we got were good ones.

26

Leeds v. Manchester United. Their 2–2 draw in the championship was, for United, the League match of the season. Their F.A. Cup meeting spanning five hours in all, decided by the only goal of the whole contest, was very probably *the* match of the season.

MANCHESTER UNITED (Wilf McGuiness): I think it was the match on the Monday night after we'd played Manchester City in the F.A. Cup and after a round of the F.A. Cup on the Saturday. We'd played Manchester City and had to go all out for 90 minutes, and Leeds had a comfortable win against Sutton. We played Leeds at home here, and we didn't have Georgie Best at the time, but it was such a tremendous game—we kept going full out for 90 minutes and 2—2 was a very satisfying result, really. After a hard game on the Saturday we kept pace with Leeds who are known for their strength and team-work and fitness. As the game went, it was one of those tremendous games that nobody deserves to lose. I felt proud of the boys. I'm sure Don Revie felt proud of his lads as well. It was one of those games.

*   *   *

STOKE CITY (Tony Waddington): If there was one result I would go for this season it would be the 3—3 draw at West Ham—having the previous season gone through the same experience of being three goals down at half-time, and ending up beating them 4—3. Incredible, really. I show the film of this game pretty often, and it depends on my mood, whether I show the first half, for mistakes, or whether I show the second half where we score four goals. Anyway, here we were again this year losing 0—3 at half-time, and we pulled back to 3—3 and in fact in the last minutes of the game hit the underside of the cross-bar —and the boys maintain to this day that the ball was over the line and we'd actually won 4—3. Three goals is an awful lot of goals to be down. Getting them back and virtually winning *again* . . . It must be memorable, surely.

*   *   *

ARSENAL (Bertie Mee): I think the most satisfying League game to me was winning away at Liverpool, 1—0. To take two points out of Liverpool, at Liverpool, takes a fair bit of doing, and you get a tremendous sense of achievement. We played well, we deserved to win, and one was happy about the performance. Outside of that, the other memorable game for me, for slightly different reasons, was playing in the Fairs Cup at Lisbon and drawing 0—0 away from home. It was a good result, as results go—though we got many other good results during the season, in that we scored a lot of goals on occasions—but in this game I was looking for the future and I wanted to stabilise things. The team did stabilise, and play well. After having had a very rough period, this was sort of the start of their come-back. One got a lot of satisfaction and confidence out of that result.

MANCHESTER CITY (Joe Mercer): From the beginning of the season we were working for a better balance. We wanted to achieve a little more stability in our defence without taking from our positive play in our forward line; the easiest thing in the world is to play at the expense of your forward line, or at the expense of your defence—but we wanted the two. We worked at this, and I thought we reached fair perfection when we beat West Ham 4—0 at West Ham. From then on we were plagued with injuries, but at that time we had reached a peak. We got a 4—0 reward for it, and the reward of the way we did it. This is what we work for: method and technique and execution. There's more satisfaction from that than the sheer result. Results, really, are secondary.

*   *   *

TOTTENHAM HOTSPUR (Bill Nicholson): It wasn't a very brilliant season for us. Some matches might have been pleasing for a while, but . . . I suppose for satisfaction all through the game it might have been the match at Burnley early in the season. The fourth match of the season, and we won it 2—0. I would think that, from the point of view of teamwork, being satisfied with everybody's performance, that would be about it. One of those matches where everybody worked hard, it was effort and teamwork—added to that it was an away match—it gave a great deal of satisfaction.

WOLVERHAMPTON WANDERS (Bill McGarry): I think we probably played as well against Tottenham in the League Cup and in the championship as any game we played in the season. I think the spectators and everybody thought that, although it was only a 1—0 win for us, down there in the League match. We played very, very well, and we scored a hell of a goal—David Wagstaff went down the line and crossed the ball, and Hughie Curran came in, he'd run 50 yards, knocked it in like a bullet. These are the things that stick in your mind. We played well there for the whole 90 minutes, and played progressive football, and it brought us a goal. These are the little bits of satisfaction that managers get—especially when you have a season where you only get four points in the last two and a half months!

*   *   *

CRYSTAL PALACE (Bert Head): Strangely enough, I think the most satisfying match to a certain extent was a loss against Everton. We went up there early in the season, and at that time Everton were on top and had won well two or three games away. We opened up, one in front, we were 1—1 at half-time, and then eventually we lost on a penalty. But as far as the boys satisfying you, it was a great display. Our boys haven't finished champions —theirs have. Looking back on it, it was a great game.

29

BIG JACK AT THE BACK

Big Jack at the back is now 35. He's been playing league football since he was a teenager, and all of it with Leeds United. Such massive experience is unequalled in the league. He's also been a registered coach since the age of 20. Here, Jack Charlton talks about his age and what experience means to his game now . . .

They make me feel my age, the lads do, when they start taking the mickey, pinching my passport when we go abroad, to sneak a look. Actually, they help to keep me young.

I think my temperament's changed a bit, on the field, over the last 18 months or two years. I used to be a bit of a shouter and a moaner. I got on everyone's back. I've always been very honest with myself, and I'll criticise other people pretty easily. I don't like other people to criticise me, though. There's a bit of a quirk in my nature in that way. Before, I think I knew a little bit more about the game than some of the lads who were coming into the side at that time. And I probably showed it a little bit too much. Now they've probably learnt a bit more about the game, and I don't need to get at them as much as I did then.

I'm a lot quieter than I was then, and I control myself better—not allowing myself to go into bad positions. There's one thing, though; that I've always been proud of, and that is that I can concentrate like nobody I know—following the play, and the play off the ball—I can be oblivious to everything that's going on. I think I'm a better player under pressure. Early on, I think I tended towards picking up bad habits from skilful players whom I admired. But I found that to play a defensive position you can't afford any flannel at all. You can't afford any over-elaboration. I found a long time ago what I could do and what I couldn't; what is right for the team and what is wrong for it. It's knowing what limits you can play to.

I'm not playing as well as before, I wouldn't say. I'm playing with better players who are doing more work for me, in effect. It's more brain work now. I think there's a lot of experience in my game now. I've learnt to pace myself, so I can get through most games these days without breaking sweat. As far as Leeds is concerned, the games keep getting easier for me.

THE ROCKET FIRERS

It's a common enough sight to see a player drop to the deck and stay there—and a fairly uncommon one to see his captain come across and tend to him, like Rugby captains do. How involved, then, are captains in their job and with their team? Obviously, attitudes vary according to individual personality. Here, six such personalities talk about the way they personally see the role . . .

Dave Mackay (Derby)

You can't have a good team unless you've got a good captain or a good manager; one of the two has got to be very good. I always feel that players have got to play *for* somebody in the club. When I was with Hearts it wasn't so much the manager I was playing for so much as the trainer, Johnny Harvey, who's now the manager there; I had great respect for him, when I was playing, I was playing for him, you know. I think you've got to be popular. You can be too hard and you can be too soft; the more popular you are the better captain you'll be. On the park everybody knows more or less exactly what they're going to do, but you still need somebody out there. You do see captains who wouldn't bother to say anything—but if it was one of mine who needed something saying to I would go over and give him a whack—I would, if it was necessary . . . You can settle people down by what you do, too. If necessary, I would bring the ball down in the box and do something—I think I'm a calm player if I've got the ball and I'm using it. I wouldn't do it for show, but if people were getting panicky and the moment was right I would bring the ball down in the box and maybe push a little square one and start something away from there, something like that. Then I'm sure people would be inspired and encouraged. The same way that I get inspired by other people in the team.

32

Brian Labone (Everton)

Obviously, the captain doesn't have as much authority as he did 10 years ago. Football is such a fine art now that everything's worked out before the game. And also, it's very hard to get involved in something out on the right wing about 70 yards away. You've got to rely on players to use their own judgement, calm themselves down. But there is the sort of captain who goes around shaking his fist and shouting off the top of his head, and there's the sort like Bobby Moore, like myself, who try to lead by example. If you're doing your own job to the best of your ability that seems to be able to settle down the team. I think that the more placid I am this might just spread to the defence. Calmness spreads like panic does.

Frank McLintock (Arsenal)

Well, you know, there's different ways of showing example—and even if I'm having a bad game I always try to keep going as hard as I can so as to encourage everyone else. I get very involved, actually, and I suppose that's something to do with being made captain in the first place—because I always did it naturally, I was always shouting, and walking about and trying to encourage and give somebody a wee word or a pat on the back. And now I always try and make a point of shouting across the field, no matter how far away, if someone's done something really well—whether a forward's made chase, made a tackle, something like that—I always try to make a point of saying 'Well Done', or to get a teammate to tell him 'Well Done'. Myself, I think it's very important. I know that if I've done something well I like my other teammates to recognise it—and I don't think, if someone does a thing really unselfishly for the team, that it should be just passed off without recognition.

35

Bobby Moore (West Ham)

Every team sets out with a certain method to play to, but every game needs readjustment and you hope that the players are good enough to make them. The teams I've been in, brought up in and played in, have always encouraged that every player is a potential captain, and there should be 11 captains on the field, all trying to help and inspire each other. And football has become so thorough, in the preparation for matches and in training, that everybody knows what's expected of them should ever things go wrong. So they don't really need to be told, they're expected to readjust themselves accordingly. Also, I feel that if you lead by example you can always demand *as well* from your players.

BOBBY MOORE — "If you lead by example you can always demand as well."

Alan Mullery (Spurs)

The day after a match, when I get into my shop the manager is likely to say to me, 'Well you must have had a sore throat, your arms must ache'. Because, he'll say, he saw the T.V. last night and I was pointing to everybody and telling everybody what to do. Pointing and screaming at them. And he's right—I probably do have a sore throat. I do scream at people on the field. Not *abuse*. But I love screaming at people. I love to push people, I like to tell people, to boss them. Whether it helps or not I don't know.

Billy Bremner (Leeds)

Anybody who says it's no different for the captain is talking rubbish, because actually you're the boss of the game. You're taking the boss's place out there; if people are getting carried away a bit you're the one to cool them down, to tell them to knock it off. As well as giving them a gee sometimes and a rocket sometimes. It all depends on how much respect you have. I mean, there's two or three captains who have got the respect of their players, and there's a lot who haven't. But I've got no difficulties at all, and I'm playing with 11 internationals and I haven't found any difficulty at all in my instructions towards them on the park. And the same thing if I put a ball wrong, they're the first ones to turn round and tell me.

WHO WOULD YOU CHOOSE?

An invitation to Fourth Division managers to go window-shopping. Who would they take, given a free gift of anyone in the League? The winner was predictable, though George Best got the nod from no more than seven managers out of 24. The character of Charlton and Bremner was much admired, with four and three votes respectively. Another fancied 'team-man'—Colin Bell, with two votes. The other choices: Ron Davies, Jimmy Greaves, Johnny Haynes, Norman Hunter, Jon Sammels, Allan Clarke, Alan Hudson, Geoff Hurst. The outstanding omission: Peter Osgood.

Ernie Shepherd (Southend United)

I'm all for skill and courage, myself, and George Best has this. He has the ability to get goals from nothing. For one player he can do so much on his own—especially when, if you're playing to a system, the system isn't working out.

Jimmy McGuigan (Chesterfield)

There's so many, I don't know. But I think the complete fellow, really, is Bobby Charlton—good footballer, makes them, scores them. A terrific example to everyone around the club I would think. This would be my choice. I would think, actually, that Charlton greatly surpasses many others.

Don McAlman (Bradford Park Avenue)

Billy Bremner. As far as I'm concerned I think Billy's a pure professional, his approach to the game is terrific and he instils a hell of a lot into people around him. As a person I think it just oozes out of him, and I think the other players in the Leeds United team pick this up from him.

Jim Iley (Peterborough United)

I would take Jimmy Greaves any time. He can do what no other player in British football can do, possibly with the exception of Georgie Best now, which is to get goals consistently. To get them out of nothing. To have a player like this on your side is a big advantage today when you've got

42

Jimmy Greaves: It depends where you want the fellow to work. If he's a goal-scorer he's got to do it in that penalty box.

tight-packed defences. A lot of people throw at Jimmy Greaves that he doesn't work hard—well I always think it depends where you want the fellow to work. If he's a goal-scorer he's got to work inside that penalty box, and if he's doing his job in there for me, I don't care what he's doing for the rest of the game—because at the end of 42 games per season he'll come out with 20—30 goals. When Jimmy Greaves is finished with all the other clubs he can come down here any time and he'll still get a living with me.

Dave Bowen (Northampton Town)

I'd take George Best. There's always room for a player like that. Everybody's steeped in theory at the moment, and it all becomes a bit nondescript, it's a mid-field battle—but the wars really are won in the penalty box, and it's players like Best who win you matches, in and around penalty boxes, by virtue of their ability.

Ray Yeoman (Darlington)

Billy Bremner. He's a very professional man. George Best is an individual, but Billy Bremner is a real professional and a really good captain. He was hot-tempered when I played against him in '58 and '64, but this has all changed. He's curtailed it. I think it's really tremendous.

BILLY BREMNER (above, challenging Mullery).

"A pure professional."

". . . really tremendous how he's curtailed that temper."

"This fellow must be an inspiration to the team."

Ernie Tagg (Crewe Alexandra)

I think it would have to be Georgie Best. I think he's the greatest crowd-puller and that's what I would want. He's not the ideal footballer, but with a team like Crewe, as I say, I'd have the terraces full. If it wasn't for entertainment I would go for the ideal inside man, not necessarily a scorer of goals but one that can fetch and carry in the old style—a David Jack type of player. But there again, George Best can do that too.

Tom Johnston (York City)

I'd say Jon Sammels of Arsenal. I saw a fair bit of Arsenal when I was at Rotherham and Huddersfield—through the Cup and the League Cup—and I like watching them now. I like the style of Jon Sammels; I feel he can do a bit in mid-field and he can also score goals. Probably a more honest player than some. I feel I'd get good value from him.

Jimmy Melia (Aldershot)

I think Billy Bremner. This fellow must be an inspiration to the team, he makes everybody else play, and he wants to play himself, and he hates to get beat.

Frank Blunstone (Brentford)

The boy I would take is Alan Hudson at Chelsea. I think this boy will be a great player in time. He's a great player *now*, and he'll be better still eventually. He's only 18; in a couple of years he must be one of the best

players in the country. I would take Hudson as an investment. At the present time—just for the one season—I'd take Allan Clarke—scoring goals and looking to score goals.

Dick Graham (Colchester United)

The player who's scoring the most

goals [Allan Clarke], because that's what we need. Someone who can get goals, that's what the game is all about. The question is what we want at the moment, and that's what. It's a wonderful question that, because it could never happen. We wouldn't be able to afford his *train fare*.

John Frizzell (Oldham Athletic)

Probably I would go for George Best, without any second thoughts.

Ken Roberts (Chester)

Do I need to say? Bestie. When we talk about individual players this is the one.

ALAN HUDSON. "He's only 18. He's a great player *now*."

Gordon Lee (Port Vale)

That's an easy question to answer. Bobby Charlton. I think he's the best player we've produced for a good many years, and will ever produce. Having played against him, as a defender for the Villa, I would say that he's the best footballer I've ever seen or played against. He's not only a player of ability, but I admire him because of his influence of character. He does give me the impression that he really is playing for *Manchester United*. He gives me the impression that he has the ability to be more of a brilliant individual but he does do the thing simply for the rest of the team rather than himself.

BOBBY CHARLTON

"The best footballer I've ever seen or played against."

"...greatly surpasses many others."

Bob Ferguson (Newport County)

I'm thinking of my own side, and I'm thinking of Hurst up front, because we're lacking a good mobile target man — and Hurstie's about the best in the First Division. And you'd always find him when you were in trouble at the back. Although he's a big strong lad he's all around the field, and he never pulls out; he's got a great temperament, a marvellous temperament.

"This is dedication and tremendous character."

Jimmy Sirral (Notts County)

This is just hypothetical. This is Christmas tree stuff. I don't know that I admire anybody's ability. I just don't know all these people — the only way you can admire people is by working with them and knowing what makes them tick. I like to watch certain players, but I don't know that I admire any player . . . I am canny yes. I have to be canny. I have to be humble. This is what the game is all about.

48

John Neal (Wrexham)

George Best—I've played against and watched him, and admired this fellow. He's got so much flair, which is what you need; it's unusual. He's a genius, this boy, a real genius, and he's still learning.

Another one I would take would be Norman Hunter, I suppose I might be the only one, but I would do that. You don't hear Norman Hunter mentioned a great deal, but this chap's a fabulous professional. He does the job at the back so well, he destroys so well, he's so strong, he reads the game so well, he's got the best left foot in the game. He's ruthless—but fair—and this is how the game should be played, with this fellow's approach.

Ron Ashman (Scunthorpe United)

I would take Ron Davis of Southampton. I think he's a terrific all-round centre-forward, and they're few and far between in this country—strikers, as they get called all the time today—but to me, this man's got everything. You'd be hard put to find anybody to match him in the air, and this fellow's improved so much on the ground it's amazing.

GEORGE BEST

"For one player, he can do so much on his own."
"When we talk about individual players this is the one."
"... a genius, and he's still learning."

Angus McLean (Hartlepool)

I'd take the fellow from Manchester United. Bobby Charlton. To me he's got all the football skills, and he's a chap that you could put on a pedestal and hold up as an example to any young apprentice. The ideal choice, both on and off the field.

John Newman (Exeter City)

Colin Bell, I think, probably. Not only is he a good player, but potentially a great player. People often look at players—especially in the lower divisions—from an ability point of view, but this is a great player and he's also a tremendous worker; he seems to have attributes of character which contribute to this. Because of it, he strikes me as a player that can only get better and will get better.

Brian Doyle (Workington)

I think for me—Georgie Best. It's comparatively easy to build a defence, if you have the material, and if I had Georgie Best then I could spend a few bob on defenders, spend less money and get better players—because forwards always cost more than defenders. George Best would be ideal. I wouldn't mind having him for a month, just for a loan—that would do me, we'd have some gates then.

Ron Gray (Lincoln)

I always respect Bobby Charlton. I admire this chap in many ways; this is dedication and tremendous character. He can play it and by Jove he can finish it. And his workrate is tremendous. A young kid around here, I said to him—'If you want someone to follow, take the train fare, go and watch this fellow.' What tremendous dedication. Oh, tremendous.

Bobby Kennedy (Grimsby Town)

At the moment I think it would be Colin Bell. I think he's the equal of any of them. He's got everything in his favour. He's one of the fittest players in the game and he's very skilful as well. He's up, and back; there's nothing more you can ask. He's the ideal manager's player. I think Colin could play anywhere else as well. An ideal team player.

Roy Bentley (Swansea City)

You'd have to assess who's going to be that great an asset for you *in the Fourth Division*. You've got to have the type of player that can adjust himself to Fourth Division football, which is considerably different from First Division. He's got to be someone who not only plays well but lifts other players, and there's not many of them around. There's very few that can change the game themselves—they can change it by scoring a goal, but they can't change the pattern of play. But Johnny Haynes was for me a player who could do this. He could control the pace, he could step the pace up, he could split defences wide open; he never necessarily had to score goals to change a game. He's the sort of player who could do the same in the Fourth Division.

BILLY BREMNER'S TEMPER

In looking for character in a player, no evidence of it seems as clear and as admirable as that in a man who can be seen to have come to grips with himself. This is what obviously impressed Fourth Division managers—concerned as they are, and as any manager must be—with the need to prevent players' quick temper spoiling the game and spoiling their own contribution. Billy Bremner comments on that big change in his life . . .

I have altered, but actually it hasn't been a difficult job for me. On the contrary, quite easy. I just sat down one day after the Fulham game and I realised I wasn't doing the team any good. They'd had enough bad publicity then, and I was giving them even more. I just realised I *had* to buckle down. The Boss had a few words with me. Not to the extent of really tearing a strip off or anything, but more sort of putting me right, telling me I had to steady down. It didn't come naturally, but after about six months without any trouble it just started to go right. In the last two or three years I've had only two cautions.

I think the thing that worried the Boss, and it worried me, was—would it affect my game? Would taking this element out of my game, as it were, make me lose something that was to my advantage? You know, lose a bit of sting. But it never affected me, in fact I think I've only got better. Now that I've cut out this stupidity I'm sure I've improved as a player.

FOURTH DIVISION CHOICE

To what extent do managers down in the Fourth Division 'follow' First Division sides? Who would they choose to see on Match of the Day? Do they admire the side that plays most attractively, or admire success? The answers show overwhelmingly that success, born of 'professionalism', is a virtue in itself. Almost everyone mentioned Leeds United. Also apparent were the strains of loyalty in managers who originated from 'Geordie' country. Here is what certain of the managers had to say (the conversations were held towards the end of the season).

THE MECCA

Don McAlman (Bradford Park Avenue)

The team I admire most of all at the present time is Leeds United. Very consistent. Everybody can learn from watching this team. *Everybody*. To go there, into that environment, must be a very wonderful thing.

THE KOP

Gordon Lee (Port Vale)

I think supporters are very important, and I'm sure that's been a considerable part of the success that Liverpool and Manchester United have had. I think they're very good supporters, especially Liverpool's. I've watched on T.V. when Liverpool played two away matches in the Cup—they weren't winning, but the volume of encouragement they gave away from home was very great and I thought, how good for the Liverpool players.

STANDARD BEARERS

John Newman (Exeter City)

I always look for Leeds, because I admire what's been done there and the way it's been done. This is probably a team, or club, that has really been responsible for lifting the standard of League football. In six years they've achieved a tremendous amount, and they're there for everybody to hit and everybody's got to lift their standards up to them.

A team one always like to see, because of individual skills, is Manchester United, and one of the games I really enjoyed was between the City and United. These sort of Derby games, particularly between these two—you get some Derby games which are not too good as games—but these two seem to be able to lift themselves. It's not only a good game, it's also very competitive, and without ill-feeling.

54

Liverpool v. Manchester United. Not only the fans are watching. "This for me is luxury, watching teams like these," says a Fourth Division manager.

THE TOP SIX
Brian Doyle (Workington)

For admiration, looking at it coldly, I can't see anything stopping Leeds and Everton, and it doesn't surprise me when I look and see they've won or drawn away from home; I think I'd be shaken if I saw them get beaten, especially Leeds. Because they're so professional. I think that in the First Division you can more or less name, for the next season, the six teams that are going to be there or thereabouts. You know, not this season but *next* season. Again, from the professional point of view — it might not be the spectator's view — I can enjoy a 0 — 0 draw between Leeds and Chelsea, if it was to happen, because to me it would be a game of great skill; one team trying to break down the other's defences. So I suppose I'd like to watch Leeds play, if I had the choice. And Chelsea look good at the present moment — I admire the manager Dave Sexton, he's an honest professional, he's a grand lad really, he just works at his job and gets on with it. Quiet and solid, a nice fellow.

UNDERDOG VIEW
Roy Bentley (Swansea City)

Well, I always like to see Chelsea do well, being an old club of mine — they deserve honouring somewhere. But I've got a great respect for Leeds. We played them, of course, in the Cup this year, and we could have, and nearly did, bring off one of the shock defeats of all time. That doesn't diminish them in my eyes. My opinion of the game before was that we could raise our game — let's face it, it's easier for the under-dog to raise its game in this sort of situation than for the favourites. They had a bit of a shake-up against us, and this was their lesson, well-learnt, I'm sure.

PALACE REVOLUTION
Dick Graham (Colchester)

My feelings must always go with the Palace, having been with them as a player and then later as a manager — and especially, you know, remembering that they spent about 30 years getting out of the Third. I've been watching them very carefully because obviously it's been a tremendous struggle to try and survive in the First Division. If only they can stay there they'll have done a good job. It's a matter of acclimatizing and adjusting to it, isn't it? Sometimes clubs have gone right up fast and then straight back; sometimes it's been a good thing for a club to just get used to the First Division before it goes that step on.

Myself, that's the sort of team I'd like to manage, one at the bottom of the League. I think it's a greater achievement to bring a team off the bottom and eventually get success with them. I'm probably at my best doing that. Something to really get your teeth into.

"You find yourself digging and delving and critcising. You say, 'Well why didn't they succeed, this side?'" Angus McLean, manager of Hartlepool, might well have asked that question after the Cup Final, won for Chelsea with Webb's header (above).

56

T.V. CLASSROOM
Angus McLean (Hartlepool)

Well of course, I always watch Match of the Day from a scholastic point of view rather than for entertainment — and then we'll talk with the players about it, those who saw it, on the Monday or Tuesday. Being a professional in the game, it spoils watching the match, actually. You find yourself digging and delving and scrutinising and criticising. You say, 'Well why didn't they succeed, *this side?*' — you can say nine times out of ten that it's lack of professionalism. That's why this Leeds side are so good, they're so professional with it.

GAME FOR GAME
Bob Fergusson (Newport County)

I like to see West Ham win because of their attacking approach to the game, but I admire Leeds very much for their tremendous professionalism — the results show that they take it game for game, and nobody's a good player, they're only as good as the last result, but they go on proving themselves every week, and this is marvellous professional thinking. I admire Leeds, but I like to see West Ham win because they're such a nice band of attacking players there. I always like to see Manchester City, for their flowing football. I think Manchester City and West Ham would be as good a game as any to watch, an exciting and open game with a lot of tactics worth watching.

58

"You never hear Bill Shankly make an excuse when he gets beaten" – as above, when Liverpool lost to championship winners Leeds in the last game of 1969.

SHANKLY'S MEN
Ernie Tagg (Crewe Alexandra)

I played for Wolves, but I've a soft spot for Liverpool. I certainly don't think I'm biased; I think Bill Shankly is the best manager of the 92. I've talked with him and listened to him and dealt with him, and he's so genuine and fair. He's the greatest of managers. He puts everything into the game and never looks for anything out of it. He's so honest, and always got a soft spot for the losers – you never hear Bill Shankly make an excuse when he gets beaten; he's that much of a man he accepts the game for what it is. I've built a real admiration for him. So when Liverpool are on T.V. I never miss, but if someone else is on and I haven't got the time it doesn't worry me. I tell you, I wish I could get my lads playing the same as Liverpool.

THE PUIR DIVILS
Jimmy Sirral (Notts County)

Should we admire First Division teams? Too busy doing my own job. The only teams that you like to see winning are teams that your friends are working for. You know, you say 'that puir divil's in trouble this week' or, 'I'm glad that they won this week.' The successful teams? Well, you might think, 'They're doing well this year, wonder how they'll do next year.' But I don't know. I don't admire anybody in football.

59

THE FABULOUS FIRST
John Neal (Wrexham)

I admire them all. I admire them for where they've got to, the thoroughness with which they've approached it, I think it's fabulous. I visit a few of these clubs; I was up at Crystal Palace the other week, and this is a great set-up. I admire it. I'm jealous of it in fact. There's been a tremendous amount of work go into these clubs to build them up the way they are, and they're still building and working, and this is how I'd like to see Wrexham going.

I enjoy watching any First Division side. People say of Leeds that they aren't a very attractive side—but I don't think so, I enjoy it. What I term a luxury trip is when I've watched these teams. None of the responsibility of hunting for players as I do when it's Central League or Combination football, Reserve team or non-League, where I spend most of my time. When it's a First Division match this is a luxury trip for me, and it's just a case of what I can learn, tactically; this is what I like about it.

When the results come through, the one I'm always looking for in the First Division is for my home town, Sunderland. I lived in a small pit village on the outskirts of Sunderland for 17 years of my life, 20 years ago, and this is the team I'm still interested in. I don't know any of the players or anybody connected with the club, and I still take a very keen interest in the club, and I still get the *Sunderland Echo* sent up every week to keep abreast of the times there.

THE PRODUCTION LINE
Jimmy McGuigan (Chesterfield)

I think there is always a tendency to admire teams that are doing consistently well, and Leeds readily spring to mind—highly organised, the conveyor belt, the production line, has been very good for years now ... Leeds v. Chelsea, Leeds v. Manchester United—any of these would be very attractive fixtures for a manager to see on T.V. But there's something to be learned even from a team that's not pulling together. You can learn a great deal from that.

WEEK IN, WEEK OUT
Jim Iley (Peterborough United)

I think the first result I look for after ours is Newcastle's. I played for a lot of other clubs, including Spurs and Forest, but the only one I'm really interested in is the one where I enjoyed my football most, and that's Newcastle. Outside of that, I would say definitely Leeds. Leeds or Liverpool. These are the teams with method, they play to the system—they just don't go out, for instance, like Spurs, and turn it on one day and not the next. They go out there 42 games in a season and they grind you down—it's the same every week, week in and week out.

Continued on page 62 ▶

60

FOURTH VS. FIRST

Brian Doyle (Workington), on the difference between *FOURTH AND FIRST*

I think football is basically the same, in that in all divisions you're all trying to play the same type of football—it's variations on a theme, more or less. I know I roast my players for certain mistakes. I say, 'Well you should have had more sense than to do that, that was stupid'—and then I look at Match of the Day, and the top fellows have made the same mistakes. Then you say to yourself, 'Well, if I was with that club I would have to roast them as well.'

What you see, really, when you look at a First Division side, are better players, individually, playing collectively. Probably sharper in mind, these fellows, as well as in speed. Speed of thought is the big thing in the First Division. In a lower division you can have the teamwork, you can have the willingness to run, the same type of plan, basically. But what they've got, probably, is a little more skill in the brain. Whereas I might have three or four players out of 11, they will have nine out of 11, who are fairly good thinkers—which makes up, in some cases, for lack of speed. They talk about Pat Crerand being slow, but he's such a quick thinker. Another fellow can be a greyhound, but dead slow upstairs; they're not in the same street.

Manchester United and Chelsea: two of the star teams and only one can be a winner. "I admire them all," says one Fourth Division manager. "I don't admire anybody in football," says another.

ALL-WEATHER CHAMPIONS
Ernie Shepherd (Southend United)

I follow Leeds, particularly with Don Revie being an old club-mate of mine at Hull. I think Leeds are so very, very professional, with so many good players. To me, they're the best all-round side in the country—they can play on the frosty, bone-hard grounds that need players with courage, and on the lush-top they've got the skill.

FOOTBALL VIRTUE
Dave Bowen (Northampton Town)

I like to see Arsenal do well, certainly, having been with them for 11 years. Being manager of the Welsh international side I like to see lots of teams do well that have Welsh international players in. But by and large I like to see teams do well that deserve to do well, by virtue of their hard work, their desire to play, their application, the skill factor. I can look at a match on television which may be fine to other people but to me it's like reading a book and getting to page 12 and there's something wrong with the plot. There's so many teams, I feel, that have pleasant results which are completely ungenuine; and there's the kind of side that's very high in our rating and goes somewhere and gets mutilated — but it doesn't happen for long. They get back on the winning trail. This is what I'm interested in.

FOR DON REVIE, WHERE IS THE SUMMIT?

We've reached one peak now, that we've got to improve on. I think we've matured in the last two years. We had been a very consistent side with a lot of ability and a lot of method, and now we've blossomed out as an attacking side, we've played some great attacking football, home and away, and with all this tremendous ability in the side it's an exciting team to watch. But we've reached a peak that we'd been heading towards for six or seven years. To improve that peak, it's going to be a slow movement now. Nothing sudden. We've just got to work even harder at everything we do: our basic skills, our tactical moves, everything, to be the great side that we want to be.

I've played with five clubs, with five different outfits and managers, and I don't think I've ever come across a set of players that would die for each other — not only on the field, they'd help each other off it too. And I'm sure that if they keep on working and wanting to learn, that they could go down as one of the greatest sides that ever lived.

FACES
IN
FOOTBALL

LES GIBBARD, Guardian cartoonist,
looks at selected football stars with the
eye of a caricature artist. In quick, "30-
second" sketches, Gibbard seized on the
"main points I would go for in a face"
and then talked clinically about those
features.

This is an almost skull-like face of Charlton's. I don't suppose he would like to be called that, but anyway he's obviously balding; and his forehead bulges out considerably at the top and then comes out into quite a bridge above the eyes. His eyes are very sort of watery and almost non-existent in a way, not the essential feature at all, you could almost draw him without eyes. They're very deep-set and pale.

The thing about Georgie Best is his heavy eyebrows—very dark around the eyes. And his mouth, it draws back as though he does all the breathing out of the side of the mouth, and, obviously, here is a main feature. Once again, deep-set eyes—in fact sometimes you get the impression he hasn't got any eyes, there's so much shadow underneath, with those bushy eyebrows.

Dougan is all eyebrows and a piercing look. His eyes and his eyebrows seem to meet, piercing little eyes just underneath the eyebrows. A very long nose. I drew him more or less as an upside-down triangle, because his whole face seems to slope down to a point, and you can't even see the chin as such. He's a downward-facing man who looks up through his eyebrows.

66

Bobby Moore's the only round face of all these. I made him too round, almost fat, but his nose gives you that impression—it's not short at all, but it gives the impression of squatness. He's got very big, penetrating eyes. Just a suggestion of eyebrows. I don't know how to describe his lips, but they look somehow as if he gets what he wants—like *Ozymandias,* "the wrinkled lip and sneer of cold command." He looks like a thinker or a schemer.

Summerbee's is a face that sticks in the mind—a fairly prominent nose, intelligent eyes, and quite a noticeably overhanging top lip and a fairly weak under-lip. He's got a worried look—gives you the impression that he's obviously experienced the troubles of the world sort-of-thing—and that he's a thinker. A strategist.

This last gentleman, Marinello, has got very wide eyebrows—they almost meet in the middle, and they stretch right across the face to where his hair is, so there's almost continuous eyebrows straight across. He's got a perpetually open mouth. He looks quite a worried fellow, despite the smile. He's got a few signs of wrinkles.

DAVE MCKAY OR ALAN MULLERY

I just can't lose. Not even in training, in a practice match. When Dave Mackay was at Tottenham we were just head-on all the time. In all the years we played together, Dave and I, I don't think we were ever in the same 6-a-side team. The first thing the trainer used to do every morning was to get two shirts, a green one and a yellow one, and give one to Dave and one to me. That was the first thing that used to happen. He never gave anyone else a shirt before he gave Dave and me one.

I wouldn't have thought anyone could get more involved in a match than me. But I don't know — I played with Dave in a charity match this year up at Crystal Palace, and when a goal was scored against his side and he thought that someone had made a mistake that led to it, he was letting that fellow know about it, pointing and shouting and getting upset. In a friendly match, it was. A *charity* match.

WHO IS THE BETTER LOSER?

We played in the gym, and over the years there were so many battles and personal fights. I mean, you get in a gym, 6-a-side, and the only time the ball stops is when there's a goal. If you shoot for goal and the ball hits the wall and comes back it's still in play, so the game is very, very tough, it's very physical; you're all heated up, and tempers get frayed. There are numerous fights — which get stopped quickly, everybody dives in. These things happen, and I think it's easier for you to control yourself on the pitch than it is in certain training.

There were some great players there in that match and I think people paid money to come in and see them. They saw Tommy Steele on the right wing, that's fair enough, they didn't expect him to play the same. But they expect him to try and do things, to do his best. And they expect everyone else to do his best. Anything I play, I play to win. If I play with my kids, or my young brothers, I would always beat them. I'd let them score a few goals, I wouldn't beat them 10-0, but I'd always beat them. *It's the only way;* otherwise there'd be no point to it.

LIFE IN GOAL

When the Fourth Division managers went window shopping (page ''') none of them chose a goalkeeper, though that man's influence over the result of a game is as great as anyone's. The truth is that most clubs, big and small, are well served by their goalkeepers. England was undoubtedly better represented in this department than any other World Cup squad. This strange vocation seems to suit the British temperament, to produce courage and quick-thinking in the face of pressure and tension. The man whom statistics indicate to be the safest League keeper in recent years, Arsenal's BOB WILSON, here discusses his job and the photos which show it like it is . . .

YOU'RE ALL ALONE.....

I see him as a Director; directing, organising his defence. You are all alone. This photo's a good commentary on that. It shows how large the goal is, and how close the crowd is—all ready to shout, to moan or cheer.

.....AND VERY ANXIOUS

These are very anxious, panicky moments. The one with Stepney shouting is obviously an in-swinging corner. Of course you always have your own men on the post, and there they are, Law and Edwards, and it's their job when it's a near-post ball like that. Stepney is obviously shouting "Get up to it" or "Meet it"—and they are doing their job well. Even so, it's a very, very panicky moment. You're just hoping that they're going to do their job properly. The other two photos are more desperate situations. I can't say that you thrive on this sort of thing. They're not the moments you enjoy in retrospect. The moments you enjoy are when you handle clear-cut saves. These other moments are desperate, last-ditch things—but they're what goalkeeping's all about, because these are the situations when you really are the last line of defence, the ball's flying around loose, and this is where you earn your keep.

.....ALWAYS UNDER PRESSURE

The photo with Clyde Best in it is a good demonstration of the challenge you're always bound to get. A goalkeeper is always having to concentrate on the ball and the ball alone. It's no good him keeping one eye on it and the rest of him thinking about getting a knee up and how else he can protect himself. The thing is that these other fellows, they know that with your arm's reach advantage you're bound to get the touch anyway, so all they're trying to do is to knock you off balance. This is what Best is doing. Sometimes they're penalised and sometimes, if you get a reasonable clearance anyway, you'll just be allowed to play on. In the other photo, Sprake has taken the ball absolutely cleanly—his eyes are focused on the ball from just inches away—and the other fellow's there, they have no great hope of getting it really, they're throwing in as many bodies and causing as much distraction as they can. This is the thing that might just put you off a tiny little bit.

▶

.....VULNERABLE TO INJURY

This fellow swung at this, I remember it quite clearly. I can't remember exactly where he hit me—on the shoulder, I think. Especially if you go arms first and body first—head first—for blocking, you're bound to get hurt. I've broken my arm twice now. And various cuts and things—I had my ear stitched back on towards the end of this last season. I don't think of it as a stupid position. I just appreciate the ups and downs. It's very much a glory position—but you can play brilliantly for 89 minutes and in the 90th minute make a bad mistake, and everybody remembers that. When that happens, and you see the ball go into the net, it *is* real pain.

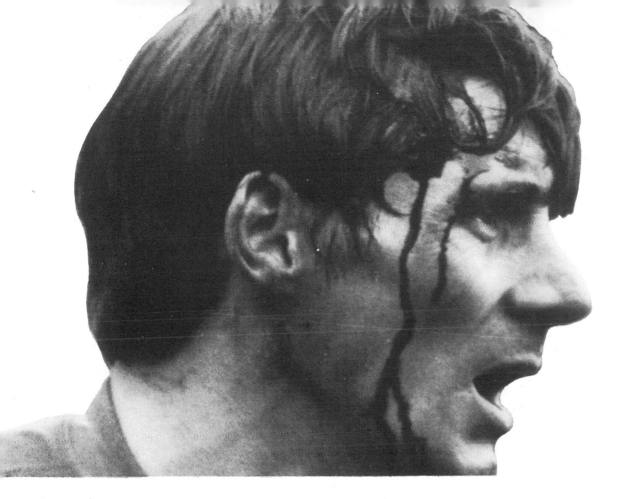

AND THE PAIN OF A GOAL

▶

.....YOU HAVE TO BE HONEST WITH YOURSELF

After the Wembley Cup Final, everybody—even Bonetti in the other goal—tried to find a reason for Sprake letting in that first Chelsea goal. Sprake didn't want a reason—he'd let in a bad goal, and he knew it. He dived wrong, in the first place, he was going down on his belly and it squeezed through underneath. Whereas if he'd done it properly and dived sideways, he didn't have to catch it, it would have hit his body and he'd have saved it. And he admitted that, he didn't want any sympathy, he knew he'd let in a bad goal. You know, basically, whether it's your mistake, or a defensive error, that's caused a goal. And then you get the times when you're beaten by something that you've just got no hope with. But you don't very often see it as unstoppable—you can usually think of something leading up to it that could have been done to cut out the danger.

.....BUT SOME DAYS ARE YOURS

When you're under a lot of pressure there's not really any problem of concentration. Your technique is working for you and there's so much nervous tension. It's impossible to be worried or nervous at that moment. You *can* feel great in a game, definitely. It doesn't even matter if the scores are close, it won't make any difference if that's the way you're feeling. It can be even the reverse of how you were feeling before you came on the field—different either way—you just don't know till you get on the field. Actually, I like a knock early on, it shakes you up, gets your senses absolutely racing, and you're on edge and suddenly alive. These are the days when you're seeing the ball twice the size, you feel that everything's going for you, and you're *not* going to be beaten on this day.

VICTIMS
OR
MARTYRS?

Rodney Marsh brought down by Dave Mackay. One might almost say, from the expression, that Marsh has been pole-axed. For a more comprehensive photographic examination of a very similar incident, see over.

This incident concerns Bonds of West Ham (tackling) and Jackson of Everton. With whom does the guilt lie, and how heavy is it?

The second photograph, if seen on its own, would suggest that Bonds has been cruelly fouled.

But the first photo, again viewed independently, would suggest nothing more than a sliding tackle and a disputation of possession.

On the other hand, it could be argued that the expression on Bonds' face throughout the three photos conveys an element of mischievousness, a suggestion, perhaps, of a certain degree of guilt.

But perhaps the most interesting comparison is that between photos 1 and 2. In the first, with the tackle already made on him, Bonds' eye is still on the ball and his expression is full of purpose. What, therefore, has happened to induce the agony which suddenly appears in photo 2? An agony, indeed, almost identical to Marsh's on the previous page – except that Marsh has time to place a hand to his wounded side.

1

THE BIG STARS?

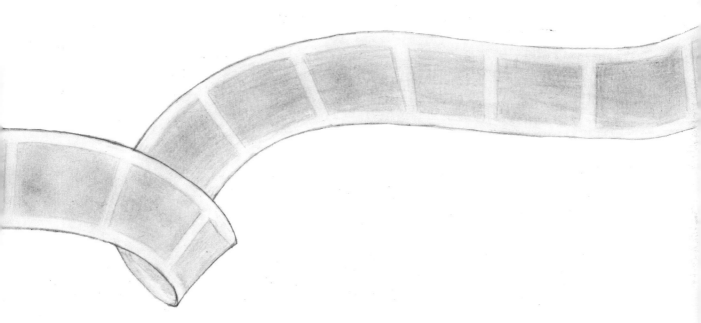

Footballing ability aside, who are the big stars of the game? What are the individual roles in which each is seen by the public? PAUL TREVILLION, an artist and a football enthusiast, is well qualified to give an interpretation: he watches the stars from where the public sees them, from amongst the crowd. With vivid imagination and some dramatic license, he talks about the game's Big Stars in terms of the stars of the screen . . .

Bobby Charlton
As
GARY COOPER

He's like an old gun-fighter, Charlton. Very reserved, very fair-minded, the good man who never gets involved in a brawl or fight. But when this man is finally provoked you know he's going to pull out the gun and kill the other guy; this man always wins. And this is Charlton, a 'goody' gun-fighter, he goes around that pitch and they knock him about and he does nothing, he never retaliates. You think, 'Well, get onto him, Charlton, why the hell don't you kick him back? What are you *doing*?' And all of a sudden — bang, the ball's in the back of the net. Or if not this game, then in the next game it is. He gets them in the end. That's the great Charlton. He's a Gary Cooper or a Randolph Scott.

George Best
As
JAMES DEAN

They feel for Charlton, they're sentimental. But with Best it's different. Best is *the* self-star. Best is *so* unobtainable. He's got it all. He's so good-looking, and the crowd, well they like him and they don't like him: he's got too much, too much going for him. Watching George Best play football is like watching someone on the cinema screen. He's always out of reach. The only way you're going to get him is writing letters to him — fan mail — something like that. He doesn't need anybody, and he shows you this. He's like Rudolph Valentino, he's like James Dean. Every girl looks at him, and you're just never going to get him. No one's going to get him. He is a real star. He's the James Dean of football.

Derek Dougan
As
DANNY KAYE

They call Dougan the Clown Prince, and this is what he is. He's like a good clown, he does something which is absolutely ridiculous—breaks a plate, spills the water—but it's so damn professional, the timing is so good. And he doesn't just throw it all in at once, he gets a laugh out of every piece. All these little circus tricks of his—these little flicks and funny overhead kicks, his jumping over the ball, catching it between his feet and flicking it behind him—he never does them in his own half of the field where they could cause trouble, he saves them for the other end of the field. He looks funny, and you laugh—until you see where the ball finishes up and the trouble it causes. He's an extrovert, he's shaven off his hair, he likes attention. He loves to make the crowd laugh. He prefers the crowd to laugh than to roar. He is a Danny Kaye, *definitely* a Danny Kaye.

Jimmy Greaves
As
CHARLIE CHAPLIN

Greaves is the little man with all the cheek. When he scores, it's always a cheeky goal off the toe. Jim'll stop, he'll puff his cheeks out, it's been an effort, but he *never* turns around after scoring a goal and runs around the pitch punching the air. You see his little eyes pop, he's happy, he'll turn around, shrug his shoulders, walk away. The job's done, the ball's in the back of the net. He's a little Charlie Chaplin. Chaplin used to be always hooking someone's chair away with his walking stick, little accidental, comical things like that—and this is Jim, the way he flicks a ball through someone's legs, and a fellow behind who Greavesy couldn't have seen comes hammering through with a hard tackle and misses him, and everyone laughs; and the way he goes and gets the ball when it's in the net and presents it to the goalkeeper, looks at the maker's name and points to it... He'd do his best work for a French director.

Bobby Moore
As
RICHARD BURTON

Of all the players today, Moore is the nearest thing to a film star. Because of his whole manner on the field; he plays the film star. He runs the show, everybody else is the supporting cast. They play to him, and they feed off him, off the lines he gives them. I sense this about Moore: that it's a personal game for him, especially when he's playing for England. If the scene's being stolen from him, then you'll see Bobby start to clap his hands, wave his arms, start to call for the ball, start moving up-field more. Every time he plays for England this is his picture, and he's got to be the star. And he is, he's the No. 1 Super Star, the boss man, the big man in town. A John Wayne, a Richard Burton. I see him in the corridors of power; he could play Wilder in *The Power Game*.

Charlie Cooke
As
CARY GRANT

Charlie Cooke is the gentleman footballer. I feel he could go out there in his best Sunday suit and play and still come in looking just as crisp and clean. Everything about him is tidy, business-like—if he starts one of his mazy dribbles, and someone tackles and the ball breaks, it's messy, it doesn't appeal to Cooke anymore. He likes to do it neat, he likes to look impressive. A lot of people make the mistake about him that he's one of these footballers who improvises, like Marsh. But he's not, he's the complete opposite. He is the matinee idol; the only man who can play football and not break into a sweat. He's the nearest thing we've got to Cary Grant.

Alun Evans
As
TOMMY STEELE

Evans is the old-time music-hall comedian. He needs the crowd. If something funny happens, Evans will turn around and look at the crowd and laugh and get them laughing. At Tottenham once, kicking in before the game, someone kicked a ball as Lawrence was getting one out of the net and it hit Lawrence, who didn't seem to think it was funny at all, but Evans laughed like an idiot and looked at the crowd, straight at the crowd. He wants them on his side, he needs them. And if he thinks they've missed something funny, he brings it to their attention. He'll replay it for them, he'll crack the same joke, repeat the punch-line. So Evans could be a comedian, he could stand up on a stage in the street. He could be a Joe Brown type of guy. A Tommy Steele.

Francis Lee
As
JAMES CAGNEY

Francis Lee, he's the tough guy. Of all the footballers today, no one sniffs or spits as much as Lee. He's got very tight lips—he's got no lips at all, Lee, he looks terribly tough. He's hungry. He'll push players out of the way, he'll kick at the ball in a goalkeeper's hands. He's a little tough guy—he harks back to Cagney. And they all love this about him; he's the sort of guy you see playing in the street. It's the tough element about Lee, terribly terribly tough, terribly strong, terribly brave. He's a man who could cut them down; he could play the gangster roles. He could carry a gun and look good. On the pitch, he should play in black leather gloves.

Peter Marinello
As
FREDDIE BARTHOLOMEW

The thing that appeals about Marinello is that he looks like a little boy, he's waif-like. He's much slimmer than Best, and he's got bigger eyes—he's throwback to one of those old Dutch paintings, one of these boys with the long hair and the little satin suit, standing on these checkerboard floors with a little dog in their arms. That's what Marinello looks like, when he comes out on the field in his little satin suit and his thin limbs—and when he gets beaten he still stands there for a minute with a long face, he looks hurt, and you think, 'God, let's get over there and help this poor lad.' He's tailor-made for the period parts. He could play all those roles that Freddie Bartholomew made his own, like the boy in *Captain Courageous*, and *Little Lord Fauntleroy* and *Tom Brown's Schooldays*.

Rodney Marsh
As

MICHAEL CAINE

Rodney Marsh could play one of these roles that Kirk Douglas always does, where the guy comes into town and you know he's going to ham it up by the end, he's going to get killed. He's a good-looking, smart-looking fellow, but somehow you're going to end up feeling sorry for him. Rodney's always getting his teammates into the most awful trouble, he gets them kicked to pieces with some of his stupid passes — then he does the most marvellous thing straight afterwards, he'll beat five men when the team's in trouble. He's a Michael Caine, he could play *Alfie*. Alfie messed it up and was doing the most atrocious things, and you felt sorry for him. *What's it all about?* That's Rodney Marsh.

Geoff Astle
As
BELA LUGOSI

If you look at football teams, they've all got young kids in them, kids that look about 18, and all of a sudden Astle comes out and he looks as if he's stepped out of 1919 — he only needs a big moustache and his hair parted in the middle and he'd look about 50. He could wear the old football gear, the long baggy trousers, the cardboard shoes with the square-cut toecaps, the big thick stockings with the padding in them — he'd look great. He's the only one who could play the horror roles, the ones you used to see old 'Beastly' Bela Lugosi in. He's so tall and dark and menacing around that penalty area. He's got those black eyes, and his black hair's like a raven's wing out of the side of his head. He ought to wear a black strip as well. He's the only one I wouldn't like to pass in the players' tunnel. I wouldn't like to see him in a floodlit match if there was a full moon.

Billy Bremner
As
MICKEY ROONEY

In every way, Bremner is another Mickey Rooney. It's the most complete comparison in football. They actually look the same, with this little turned-up nose, round face, big eyes. They're both a bit petulant. In all his films, no matter how well dressed he was, after about five minutes you'd see Rooney with his hair out of place and his shirt hanging out a bit. Same with Bremner, his shirt'll be out and he won't do anything about it. In a Rooney film, when there was fighting, he'd always go charging in against all the odds, no chance at all, but this little brave guy would jump in — sometimes he'd come out unscratched, but a lot of times too he was left laying on the floor. This is Bremner, going into that penalty area where the fires are hottest. Another thing, and they used to talk about this in the film world, when Rooney was knocked down he never got up in the conventional way — he never prised his body-weight up by putting his hand on the floor and levering with his knee, he just bounced back up. Same with Bremner, he springs up as if the grass was a trampoline. Also, Rooney was known as the perpetual chatter-box, in fact he used to almost script his own stuff, ad-lib all the way through a film. This is Bremner, the talkie footballer. And then, Rooney had this endearing habit, after doing something that really was a bit over the odds, of turning around and over-apologising. The same with Bremner — if he ever does apologise then he over-does it; he stands there and shakes his head and pats the fellow on the back and puts his hands out and he pleads and looks downwards. But he rarely apologises, the same as Rooney. They even have the same mannerism of rubbing the back of the hand across that turned-up nose. Billy Bremner *is* Mickey Rooney.

DAVE MCKAY, 35, AND BURNING BRIGHT

Dave Mackay is not only a hero, having three times recovered from a broken leg, and not only a leader, having taken Derby County further in two years than anyone could have predicted—one of the great personalities of today's game.

I'm a fiery type of player naturally; but I give my father credit for what he told me a long time ago. It was my first game for Hearts, way back around 1952, and on that particular day I had lifted my fists and was going to fight. My father said you would never get anywhere if you started picking up your hands—I've always remembered this—and I've always tried to keep them down. In my 20 years as a footballer I've only lifted my hands about four times. Considering the amount of games and the amount I get involved in games, that I'm a bad loser and I've got a very bad temper when things are going wrong—or if people are taking the mickey out of me or people are taking a kick at me . . . considering all this, I think I've done very well.

You can't possibly tell how you're going to react. But I think you've got to be enthusiastic—well, I've always been enthusiastic. It's a thing you can't pick up; you've either got it or you haven't. I've always been the type of person that I enjoy my football—especially when I'm winning! I'm definitely just as enthusiastic as I ever was, in fact more so.

The greatest moment ever in my life happened this season during the Arsenal match—the thing that really caught hold of me . . . I made a mistake, I tried to give it back to our full-back, and Radford sticks his leg out and stops it and I fall down on the goal-line. Then he's crossed it and we've only got two players to three heads, and one has to come out to Radford, and now we've only got one against three: Radford pushes it to Jon Sammels who's only about 10 yards out plum in the middle of the goal, and he's shot it. From where I am it seems to be going straight into the back of the net, and I'm lying there, angry—never got up—and I'm watching the ball and it's travelling straight and the goalkeeper never dives and I think well it's right in the corner. And then—it's bouncing back off the wall at the back of the goal, because it's gone outside the far post. As I say, I would feel that was the greatest thing, you know, that's ever happened to me in football.

108

"I'm definitely just as involved, and just as enthusiastic, as I ever was. In fact more so."

"You want more. 'You're not doing it hard enough. You ain't getting stuck in . . .' You know, if a forward gets pushed off the ball without any real challenge to fight back and get it. He doesn't *need* to push back, he just *wants* to fight back. Just to get a touch in maybe, just get the ball away."

"Probably mocking the referee. So ridiculous it's just laughable."

"This would have been for the fifth goal against Spurs . . . Not for the finish of the match, no. Actually I was a bit embarrassed, getting five against Tottenham. Naturally, I wanted to win, and would keep playing to the last minute, scoring as many goals as possible against anybody — but by the time the end came, at 5–0, it wasn't all that thrilling."

POSITIVE PLAY THE EVERTON WAY

by Paul Trevillion

Arsenal goalkeeper BOB WILSON tipped Everton to win the title on the first Sunday of the season, after they had beaten Arsenal 1—0 at Highbury. "It wasn't only their forward line that impressed me," said Wilson, "it was the way the whole side hustled us. They had this terrific strength down the middle in goalkeeper GORDON WEST, centre-half BRIAN LABONE and centre-forward JOE ROYLE."

THE THROW INTO SPACE

GORDON WEST welcomes the forward who rushes in and tries to harass him after he has saved the ball and is about to kick clear. On occasions such as these, West will move across his area, pulling that player out of position so creating space into which he can throw the ball for one of his defenders to start a quick counter attack on the opponent's goal.

DECOY RUN

Right back TOMMY WRIGHT of Everton is ever alert to sprint forward and take up an attacking position on the right wing. In the diagram Wright has hit a square pass to the right half. This is the signal for the outside right to start his decoy run and move inside as if to collect a pass and in doing so pull the left back out of position. Wright, working on the blind side sprints down the touchline to receive the pass and go for goal.

THE LOFTED CLEARANCE

BRIAN LABONE will often relieve pressure on the defence with a lofted clearance over the heads of the oncoming attackers. The value of this pass is two-fold. The lofted pass, in a packed penalty area, is a far safer ball than one along the ground as it cannot be intercepted en-route.

PLAN TWO MOVES AHEAD

JOE ROYLE is adept at heading a ball across a defender to a colleague before turning quickly and racing on to collect the return pass. The secret here is that Royle thinks two moves ahead, first where to head the ball and then where to run in order to collect the quick one-two in space.

DEFENCE SPLITTING PASS

COLIN HARVEY. In the diagram, Harvey, an exceptional passer, has slipped the ball (between A and B) to a colleague and in doing so has put two defenders out of the game. The less gifted player might have tried the more obvious pass by hitting it out of the reach of C which would have meant the person collecting the ball being immediately challenged by defender D.

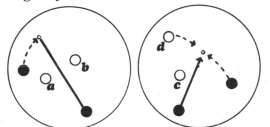

ATTACK-MINDED

HOWARD KENDALL. In the diagram Kendall has positioned himself far enough from the player to intercept the pass and yet near enough to get in a tackle should this not be possible.

The interception on, Kendall moves at top speed to take the ball through the space between the two inter-passing players and go for goal.

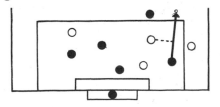

HUMAN MAGNET

When in possession in an attacking position, ALAN BALL is highly skilled at threatening to take on an entire defence. Like a human magnet he will draw defenders to him until the time is right to push the ball down the wing to a full back striking from behind. The full back will now clip the ball into the free space which Ball has created.

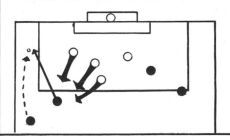

SHOOT ON SIGHT

Sharp shooter ALAN WHITTLE figured prominently in Everton's run-in for the title, scoring in six successive matches. Speed and surprise are the vital ingredients of Whittle's goalscoring flair. When a goal opening shows, Whittle wastes no time in letting fly. In some cases he is slightly off balance and does not get all his weight behind the shot. But the surprise element catches the defence on the wrong foot and puts the goalkeeper into all sorts of trouble.

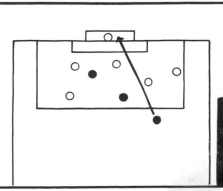

HOW IAN URE FELL, AND LANDED

Manchester United, that team of outright individuals, got hold of another one last year. Ian Ure, 29 years old and out of favour at Arsenal, wasn't perhaps the obvious choice for a team like United. In another way he was, and whereas before he had looked slightly out of place at Arsenal, he now fitted into place at Manchester with other diverse personalities like Best, Charlton, Crerand, Sartori. The choice of Ure surely says something about United. Here, Ure talks about himself 'before and after' . . .

I've been much more relaxed in my play since I've been up here. The difference is in attitude. I don't feel there's the same pressure, that the game's quite so serious. I don't feel that I'm being restrained or anything, I feel that I'm playing the game I want to play. I'm absolutely delighted at the move, it's worked out so well.

Arsenal was a very good club, but there was a hell of a strain mentally. Everyone felt it—it wasn't just myself. Most of the team were this way. It was almost too much to bear. I just feel that a goal's not the be-all and end-all

it was made out to be. I still think I was as professional a player as Arsenal ever had, in my attitude to the game. I had a few mother-and-father rows with the management, and I don't think they liked my arguing with them too much or trying to be an individual too much, and they decided that I was getting the push.

I wasn't in favour, but I think I was playing very well. I thought last season was my best of the six I'd had with Arsenal—up until the League Cup final. In fact, I thought I played very well in that game, but I made that one

ON HIS FEET

bad blunder, which was highlighted out of all proportion. And then, of course, I blundered again soon after against Leeds. It was only in the last three games or so that I found myself out of the team. I don't think Arsenal would have considered selling me before that last fortnight, I think they were more than pleased: up until then the Arsenal defence had lost only about 21 goals, which was the best in the country at that time. Things change like that in football. One minute you're king of the castle, the next minute you're a mug.

Manchester United obviously knew I was available as I was out of favour at Arsenal, they needed a defender at the time, and I was very flattered that they picked on me. I'd heard rumours in the last two years that they were interested, but I would have thought it was a bit too late for them to be coming for me. But they did come, and I've been very happy.

There's just a more relaxed attitude all around, everyone's just a wee bit freer and easier than we were at Arsenal. Arsenal's was a very rigid, stereotyped sort of game: ours is more

sort of off-the-cuff, in preparation for the game *as well* as during the game. And, apparently, it's been even more relaxed in the past. Seemingly, this year things have stiffened up a wee bit with regard to discipline and everything—and if that's so it amazes me, considering the success they had in the sixties. If things were more relaxed a few years ago, then you say to yourself, 'Is it absolutely necessary, total dedication and discipline?'—and all the things you tend to think are the way to success.

It suits me very well. They just don't know how to play a defensive game, United, they're purely an attacking team. I don't think once this year the manager's come and said, 'Right lads, today we're playing so-and-so and we're going to try and hold them to a draw, try and get a goal quick and then hold on to it.' There's none of that at all. They just don't know how to defend. It's just a nice attitude to the game—it's perhaps none too professional, but it's a nice way to play it. And you've got so many good individual players you can get away with it—I think that's the secret.

It's not a tragedy when a goal's scored against us here, that's what I like. There's no feeling of 'Well that's the game now that we're two goals down.' Because they're always liable to go and score three and make up for the two we've lost. No one ever comes in off the field and points at the goals against us. It's the way *we* play that we look to, rather than how we should play the opposition. There's no great emphasis on particular plans and things like that. We do discuss how we're going to play a particular team and how we think we should try and counteract their strength, but there's no great emphasis on this, and we don't do it for every game. There's only one way to put it: each one of them thinks, as a team, that the policy is to be attacking, to be an attractive team.

Ian Ure up in attack for Manchester United against Tottenham—"It's a nice attitude to the game—it's perhaps none too professional, but it's a nice way to play it."

THE GAMES' BAD NAME

Within weeks of the start of the new season, football was staggering under a landslide of criticism. Derek Dougan had been sent off for swearing at a linesman, and two Fourth Division players had been given the toughest suspensions ever (8 weeks)—measures which were described by an angry Professional Footballers' Association as "vicious". On the other side, the Football Association could point to the number of cases which were coming before its Disciplinary Committee, an increase of 40 per cent on the rate for the previous 12 months ... Gradually, the hubbub faded. By the end of the season Foul Play and Discipline had almost ceased to be a talking point. Perhaps the season had seen an important victory gained—a victory not just for discipline but for Football.

KINGS OF THE SCOTTISH CASTLE

CELTIC SPIRIT

"Celtic's a great organisation, and there's always the spirit there. It's the *Celtic* spirit. The team has the Scottish spirit. Celtic's always been a great team, a great club, always feared and never beaten until the final whistle." — Bill Shankly.

Rangers' Alex McDonald in firm-footed possession against Billy McNeil. But the ball, otherwise, has been running all Celtic's way.

No one at Celtic likes scoring an own-goal against Rangers, even less being congratu-lated for it — as Jim Craig is here.
Craig, and Celtic, channelled their fury into scoring goals at the other end, and ended up winners by 3 — 1.

A determined Bobby Lennox disputes possession with Leeds' Eddie Gray.

NATIONAL PROBLEMS

"You could say that Celtic ought to play for Scotland — they said the same when we had the good Tottenham side, and after we'd won the double we went out and beat England 3-2, playing comfortably — and they often say that Scotland should play only home Scots. When Scotland get beat they usually say, 'Kick out the Anglos and let's have an all-tartan XI.' I think that's a load of rubbish, really." — Dave Mackay.

Murdoch smashes his first shot at the Leeds goal and clinches a European Cup Final place.

THE CENTRAL FEUD

"The Celtic—Rangers rivalry is a good thing in one way and a bad thing in another. They're the people who *really* make the Scottish league, there's no doubt about that, as far as crowds are concerned. I spent nearly 10 years there, but going to Morton lets you see the other side of Scottish football—spectators bypassing a re-play in Greenock to go and watch Rangers and Celtic."—Bobby Collins.

THE
CUP
FINAL

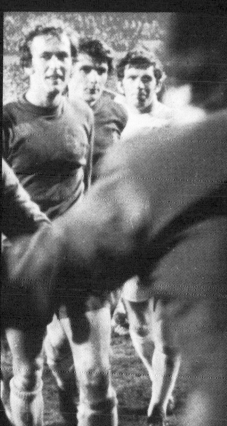

ALARUMS . . . . .

1   **2**   **3**

Tackle by Cooke on Bremner.

4   **5**   **6**

AND EXCURSIONS

1

2

Jones's challenge on goal, from which Bonetti emerged injured.

3

4

Clarke had started it by fractionally beating three men in succession. Jones finishes it by bursting past McCreadie and shooting home convincingly.

1

2

5

6

LEEDS MADE

3

4

7

8

THE GOAL THAT CHELSEA STOLE

1

4

2   3

5   6

Osgood stole it. He was able to steal it only because he was there, because he had got up there very fast from a long way back — because the Cockney spirit in Chelsea kept them from lying down. Although at the time it simply levelled the score, this was really the goal which won the match.

PICTURES OF THE YEAR

Football the tough game. In the background a giant framework of concrete and steel, in the foreground, a tower of human strength. (Everton v. Notts Forest, Royle's attack repelled by goalkeeper Hill and Hennessey.)

PICTURES OF THE YEAR

PICTURES OF THE YEAR

PICTURES OF THE YEAR

INDIGNATION, as a posse of Blackburn players, plus referee, seek justice against Bolton forward Williams after a goalmouth incident.

EXULTATION, opposite from Hibernian players Marinello and McBride at the third goal in 3—1 defeat of Rangers.

Dave Mackay, whose enthusiasm and utter involvement kept newly-promoted Derby humming all season, in anxious joint effort with team-mate McFarland. Opposite, disputing possession from ground level (both matches against Spurs).

THE FINE ART OF LOOKING AFTER NUMBER ONE. Goalkeepers aren't permanently long-suffering, like Manchester City's Corrigan, who does the next-best thing after dropping the ball. An aggrieved Webb of Chelsea looks for witnesses.

Thanks and acknowledgements to the following, who supplied the photographs:

Syndication International
E. D. Lacey
Sport and General Press Agency
The Press Association
Scottish Daily Record
Movietone News